# Crash Course US History:
# A Study Guide of Worksheets for US History

By Roger Morante

Library of Congress Cataloging-in-Publication Date is available.

ISBN-13: 978-1-7322125-0-3

Writer: Roger Morante
Cover Design: Artwork purchased from 99Designs.com.
Cover Artist: Katerina Ntelimpalta
Editor: Roger Morante
Copy Editor: Erica Brown
Back Cover Photo: Liesl Morante
Publisher Logo: Isabella Morante

To contact the publisher send an email to the address below;
holden713@gmail.com

Additional copies may be purchased on Amazon.com or by contacting the author.

Printed in the United States of America

First printing April 2018

# Table of Contents:

The Black Legend, Native Americans, and Spaniards: Crash Course US History #1

1) Describe how the population of **Native Americans** were decimated by **diseases** in the **New World.** Include which diseases killed them.

_____
_____
_____
_____
_____
_____

2) Who were the **Zuni** and **Hopi** civilizations and where did they live?

_____
_____

3) Explain some of the differences of the **Native Americans** by the regions they inhabited during **Pre-Colombian** times. Give examples and be specific in your answer.

_____
_____
_____
_____

4) Rationalize why different groups of **Native Americans** had different **religions** from each other. (Include any similarities or differences in your answer.)

_____
_____
_____

5) How did the **Native Americans** view the concept of **land ownership**?

_____
_____

6) Analyze **class distinctions** inside of **Native American** tribes.

_____
_____
_____

7) Throw light upon why **Europeans** viewed the **Native Americans** as **noble savages**.

_____
_____
_____

8) Identify who **Juan Ponce de Leon** was and explain what was he looking for.

_____
_____
_____
_____

9) What did the **pirates** do in the region and why?

_____
_____
_____
_____
_____

10) Explain the **Spanish Inquisition** in the **Americas**. What was the problem?

_____
_____
_____
_____
_____

11) Identify what happened between the **Native Americans** and the **Spanish** in **Santa Fe, New Mexico**?

_____
_____
_____
_____
_____

12) What does the term **encomienda** mean?

_____
_____
_____
_____

13) Clarify the problem historians have when trying to understand the **perspective** of the **Native Americans** and the clash of these ideas with the **Spaniards** in the **16th Century**.

_____
_____
_____
_____
_____
_____
_____
_____
_____
_____
_____
_____
_____
_____
_____

Name_____
Period_____
Date_____

When is Thanksgiving? Colonizing America: Crash Course US History #2

1) Identify what the first **English settlers** were looking for and why?

_____
_____

2) What happened to the **English Colony** on **Roanoke Island**?

_____
_____
_____

3) Analyze the reasons for the existence of the **Jamestown Colony** in **Virginia**.

_____
_____
_____
_____

4) What happened to the first **colonists** of **Jamestown, Virginia**?

_____
_____
_____
_____

5) Scrutinize the concept of the **headright system** set up by the **Virginia Company (a joint-stock company)** and measure its effects on the **colony** of **Jamestown**.

_____
_____
_____
_____

6) How did the introduction of **tobacco** change the **Jamestown Colony**?

_____
_____

7) Decipher how the 5:1 men to women ratio affected the **Jamestown Colony**.

_____
_____

8) Briefly explain what was going on in the **Maryland Colony**.

_____
_____

9) Analyze the differences between **Pilgrims** and **Puritans**.

_____
_____
_____
_____
_____

10) Clarify why the **Mayflower Compact**, written by the **Pilgrims,** was so important.

_____
_____
_____
_____

11) Who was **Squanto**?

_____
_____
_____
_____

12) Why was the sermon of "**The City Upon the Hill**," by **John Winthrop** so important in the founding of the United States of America?

_____
_____
_____
_____
_____
_____

13) Why were **Roger Williams** and **Anne Hutchinson** banished from their colonies? Include what happened to them.

_____
_____
_____
_____
_____
_____
_____
_____

14) What other types of people founded America besides the **English**? Include how this helped to shape the future of America.

_____
_____
_____
_____
_____
_____
_____
_____
_____
_____
_____
_____
_____
_____

The Natives and the English: Crash Course US History #3

1) Identify **Chief Powhatan** and explain why he helped the **English** and **John Smith**.

_____
_____
_____
_____
_____
_____
_____
_____
_____

2) Justify the **trade** that occurred between the **Native Americans** and the **English**.

_____
_____
_____

3) Identify the problems caused by **trade** between the **Native Americans** and the **English**.

_____
_____
_____

4) Who was **Pocahontas** and what did she do that was so memorable in **United States** history?

_____
_____
_____

5) What were the repercussions of the **Uprising of 1622** of **Powhatan** warriors against the **English colonists** of **Jamestown, Virginia**?

_____
_____
_____
_____
_____

6) Why do you think **anti-Indian propaganda** was written in the **colonies**?

_____
_____
_____
_____
_____
_____
_____
_____

7) Analyze the causes the **Pequot War** between the **Native Americans** and a number of **English colonists** in **Massachusetts** in 1637.

_____
_____
_____
_____
_____
_____

8) Identify what happened to cause **King Phillip's War** in 1675 between the **Native Americans** and the **English colonists**.

_____
_____
_____
_____
_____
_____
_____
_____
_____
_____

9) How did the **Native Americans** view **English colonization**?

_____
_____
_____
_____
_____
_____
_____
_____
_____

10) Why is it important to understand why **Native Americans** resisted **English colonization**?

_____
_____
_____
_____
_____
_____
_____
_____
_____
_____
_____
_____

### The Quakers, The Dutch, and The Ladies: Crash Course US History #4

1) Explain how **Colonial America** was more popular than just the early **colonial** settlements of **Jamestown, Virginia** and **Boston, Massachusetts**.

_____
_____
_____
_____

2) By what means did the **English** take **New Amsterdam** away from the **Dutch** and rename the **colony New York**?

_____
_____
_____

3) How were things better in the **Pennsylvania Colony** in respect to the other **English Colonies**?

_____
_____
_____
_____

4) Evaluate what happened to the **Native Americans** living in **Pennsylvania** after the **Walking Purchase of 1737**.

_____
_____
_____
_____

5) What was going on in the **Southern Colonies** in the regard to **colonial slavery**?

_____
_____
_____

6) Outline the causes and effects of **Bacon's Rebellion** of 1676 led by **Nathanial Bacon**.

_____
_____
_____
_____
_____

7) Elaborate on the **English Toleration Act of 1690** decree and what that meant for **English colonists**.

_____

_____

_____

8) Analyze the **Salem Witch Trials of 1691**.

_____

_____

_____

9) Identify what was going on inside of **colonial economics**.

_____

_____

_____

10) Why do you think the colonists disliked **British colonial policy** discouraging **manufacturing** goods in the **colonies** rather than in **Great Britain**?

_____

_____

_____

_____

11) Describe how **colonial society** functioned.

_____

_____

_____

_____

_____

12) Why do YOU think people sold themselves as **indentured servants** in order to come to **America**?

_____

_____

_____

13) What was life like for **women** in the **13 colonies**?

_____

_____

_____

_____

_____

_____

The Seven Years War and the Great Awakening: Crash Course US History #5

1) Outline the economic theory of **mercantilism** and how it affected **Colonial America**.

_____
_____
_____
_____

2) What is a **tariff**?

_____
_____

3) How were **slaves** part of **British America** and the **economy**?

_____
_____

4) Identify where the **French** were in **America** and what they were doing during the **Seven Years War** (1756-1763), aka the **French and Indian War**.

_____
_____
_____

5) What did the **Ohio Land Company** do that the **French** did not like?

_____
_____

6) Evaluate the effect the **French and Indian War** had on the **economy** of **Colonial America**.

_____
_____
_____
_____
_____

7) How were the **American colonies** split up after the signing of the **Treaty of Paris** in 1763?

_____
_____
_____
_____

8) What is a **primary source**?

_____
_____
_____

9) Explain the reasons behind **Pontiac's Rebellion** (1763-1766) and include its connection to the **Proclamation of 1763**.

_____
_____
_____
_____
_____

10) Identify some new ideas that began to form after the **Seven Years War (French and Indian War)**.

_____
_____
_____

11) Explain the idea of **Republicanism** in the years just before the **American Revolution**.

_____
_____
_____
_____

12) Explain English philosopher **John Locke's** liberal views on government during the **Enlightenment**.

_____
_____
_____
_____

13) What is meant by the term, "**The Great Awakening?**"

_____
_____
_____
_____
_____

14) Analyze **American revivalist preacher Jonathan Edwards** and explain his connection to the **Great Awakening**.

_____
_____
_____
_____

15) How did **religion** change during **Colonial America**, especially after the introduction of **English Anglican cleric George Whitefield**?

_____
_____
_____

16) How did the social and political thinking change inside of the **American colonies**, right before the outset of the **American Revolution**?

_____
_____
_____
_____
_____
_____
_____

## Taxes and Smuggling: Crash Course US History #6

1) Why did the **British Government** think it was fair to **tax** the **colonists** in the Americas after the **French and Indian War**?

_____
_____
_____
_____
_____

2) Expound on the reasons why the **colonists** were angry by these new **taxes** imposed on them by the **British** government.

_____
_____
_____
_____
_____
_____
_____

3) Explain the significance of the **Sugar Act of 1764**.

_____
_____
_____
_____
_____
_____

4) Justify why the **Stamp Act of 1765** was so annoying to the **colonists** that they decided to unite.

_____
_____
_____
_____
_____
_____

5) Who were the **Sons of Liberty** and what did they achieve?

_____
_____
_____
_____
_____

6) How did **women** in the **colonies** respond to the **Townsend Acts of 1767**?

_____
_____
_____
_____

7) What happened in the trials of the **British Officers** involved in the **Boston Massacre** of 1770?

_____

_____

_____

_____

_____

8) Identify the causes and effects of the **Tea Act of 1773** on the **English colonists** in **Massachusetts.**

_____

_____

_____

_____

_____

_____

_____

_____

_____

9) Outline the response of the **British Government**. Be specific.

_____

_____

_____

_____

_____

_____

_____

10) What was the purpose of the **First Continental Congress**?

_____

_____

_____

_____

_____

_____

_____

_____

11) Why was **Thomas Paine's** book <u>**Common Sense**</u> (1776) so popular with the **colonists**, and how did it push **colonists** towards **revolution**?

_____

_____

_____

_____

_____

_____

_____

Who Won the American Revolution?: Crash Course US History #7

1) Why was the **Battle of Saratoga** in 1777 the most important battle of the **Revolutionary War** (1775-1783)?

_____

_____

_____

_____

_____

2) Identify what happened at the **Battle of Yorktown** in 1781?

_____

_____

_____

_____

3) How was the fight for freedom different for **slaves** than it was for **Continental** soldiers?

_____

_____

_____

_____

_____

4) Why did many **American slaves** during the **American Revolution** ultimately decide to go back to **Britain**?

_____

_____

_____

_____

_____

5) Point out the brutality that **American troops** committed to the **Native Americans** who fought with the **British**.

_____

_____

_____

_____

6) Explain what happened to **women** in the **Revolutionary War**.

_____

_____

_____

7) Rationalize the idea of **Republican Motherhood** and how it pertained to American **women**.

_____

_____

_____

_____

_____

8) What was revolutionary about the **Revolutionary War** (1775-1783)?

_____
_____
_____
_____
_____
_____
_____

9) Explain the idea of true **religious freedom** as it applies to the time right after the **Revolutionary War**.

_____
_____
_____
_____
_____

10) How did **Eli Whitney's** invention of the **Cotton Gin** in 1793 change the institution of **slavery**?

_____
_____
_____
_____
_____
_____

11) Identify how **John Locke** influenced **Thomas Jefferson**.

_____
_____
_____
_____
_____
_____
_____

12) What was the most novel (new) idea that emerged during the **American Revolution** and how did it change our world? Elaborate on the idea.

_____
_____
_____
_____
_____
_____
_____
_____

The Constitution, the Articles, and Federalism: Crash Course US History #8

1) Explain why the **Articles of Confederation**, the system of government set up prior to the **US Constitution**, was bad, weak, and didn't work.

_____
_____
_____
_____
_____
_____
_____
_____

2) What did the **Articles of Confederation** accomplish?

_____
_____
_____
_____

3) Demonstrate what the **Northwest Ordinance of 1787** passed by the **Second Continental Congress** provided for the fledgling United States.

_____
_____
_____

4) Paraphrase the most important reason why the **Articles of Confederation** were a complete disaster.

_____
_____
_____

5) How did the states expect to pay for the **American Revolution** (1775-1783)?

_____
_____

6) Analyze what happened during **Shay's Rebellion** in 1787.

_____
_____
_____
_____

7) Analyze the differences between the **Virginia Plan** and the **New Jersey Plan**.

_____
_____
_____
_____
_____

8) Explain what was accomplished in the **Great Compromise**.

_____
_____
_____
_____
_____
_____

9) What was the **Three-Fifths Compromise**?

_____
_____
_____
_____
_____
_____
_____

10) Illustrate how the **separation the powers** doctrine attempted to balance the three branches of government that rule the United States of America.

_____
_____
_____
_____
_____
_____
_____

11) Explain the reasons surrounding the existence of the **electoral college**.

_____
_____
_____

12) Why were the **Federalist Papers,** written by **Alexander Hamilton**, **James Madison**, and **John Jay** important to establishing the new **Federal Government** of the **United States**?

_____
_____
_____
_____
_____

13) Outline the type of government which most frightened the **Anti-Federalists**.

_____
_____
_____
_____
_____
_____

## Where US Politics Came From: Crash Course US History #9

1) Why couldn't **Alexander Hamilton** become president of the United States?

_____
_____

2) Point out the reasons why **Alexander Hamilton** was in favor of a **strong government**.

_____
_____
_____
_____

3) What type of America did **Thomas Jefferson** favor and why?

_____
_____
_____

4) Spell out why **Thomas Jefferson** distrusted **concentrated power**?

_____
_____
_____
_____

5) Outline the social, economic, and political reasons why **Thomas Jefferson** favored **France** and **Alexander Hamilton** favored **Britain**.

_____
_____
_____
_____
_____
_____
_____

6) Outline **Alexander Hamilton's 5-point plan** to strengthen the **national government**.
   Point 1:

_____
_____
_____

   Point 2:

_____
_____

   Point 3:

_____
_____
_____

Point 4:

_____

_____

Point 5:

_____

_____

7) Elaborate how it was decided that **Washington D.C.** was chosen to be the home of the **National Government** and thus became the **capitol** of the **United States**.

_____

_____

8) Break down the causes of the **Whiskey Rebellion in 1794** and how it was stopped.

_____

_____

_____

9) How did the **French Revolution** complicate **American Politics** during the **Federalist Era** (1789-1801)?

_____

_____

_____

10) Why did the **British** impress **Americans** to become part of their **Navy**?

_____

_____

11) What did Washington warn against in American politics inside his **Farewell Address**?

_____

_____

_____

12) Explain a flaw that was exposed by the election of **John Adams** as president in **1796**.

_____

_____

_____

_____

13) How did the **X,Y, Z Affair** drag the **United States** into a quasi-war with **France**?

_____

_____

_____

14) Briefly explain the **Alien and Sedition Acts of 1798** which were passed under the **Adams Administration**.

_____

_____

_____

_____

15) How did the fallout from the **Alien and Sedition Acts** begin the war between **states' rights** and **federal rights** of **nullification**?

_____

_____

_____

_____

_____

Thomas Jefferson & His Democracy: Crash Course US History #10

1) Explain what happened during the **Election of 1800**.

_____
_____
_____
_____

2) What did the passage of the **12th Amendment** to the **U.S. Constitution** accomplish?

_____
_____
_____
_____

3) Identify the best thing **John Adams** ever did for the office of the presidency.

_____
_____

4) Unravel **Thomas Jefferson's** campaign motto of "Jefferson and Liberty."

_____
_____

5) What do YOU think the most important phrase inside of the **Declaration of Independence**, "All men are created equal," actually means?

_____
_____
_____
_____
_____
_____

6) Paraphrase **Thomas Jefferson's** main ideas about government.
   A) _____
   B) _____
   C) _____
   D) _____

7) Point out why **Thomas Jefferson** favored an **agrarian** farming culture rather than an **industrial** city-style landscape.

_____
_____
_____
_____
_____

8) Throw light upon the **Supreme Court** decision of ***Marbury v. Madison (1803).***

_____
_____
_____
_____
_____
_____

9) Rationalize what the **United States** gained with the **Louisiana Purchase** in 1803.

_____

_____

_____

_____

_____

_____

10) Explain the dilemma **Thomas Jefferson** had when buying the **Louisiana Purchase** from **Napoleon Bonaparte** of **France.**

_____

_____

_____

_____

11) Rationalize why **Thomas Jefferson** had to buy the **Louisiana Purchase**.

_____

_____

_____

_____

_____

_____

_____

_____

_____

12) What was the connection between **free trade** and **Thomas Jefferson's agrarian** ideals?

_____

_____

_____

_____

_____

13) Why didn't **Thomas Jefferson's embargo** against **Great Britain** work?

_____

_____

_____

_____

_____

_____

14) Explain the **hypocrisy** surrounding the **Jefferson** presidency.

_____

_____

_____

_____

_____

_____

The War of 1812: Crash Course US History #11

1) Expand upon the reason most often given for the cause of the **War of 1812**.

_____
_____
_____
_____

2) Outline the concept of **citizenship** on the high seas around the beginning of the **19<sup>th</sup> Century**.

_____
_____
_____
_____

3) Elucidate what the **War Hawks** around 1812 were thinking, such as **Henry Clay** and others like him, and how they interpreted the **impressment** of sailors by the **British**.

_____
_____
_____
_____

4) Explain how **Canada** was perceived during the **War of 1812**.  Include why declaring war on **Canada** fit in with the **Jeffersonian** model.

_____
_____
_____
_____
_____
_____
_____

5) Analyze how **Native Americans**, such as **Tecumseh**, reacted to the Americans' **Westward Expansion** inside of the newly purchased **Louisiana Territory**.

_____
_____
_____
_____
_____

6) Who was **William Henry Harrison** and what did he have to do with the **Battle of Tippecanoe** in 1811?

_____
_____
_____
_____

7) What did **Tecumseh**, nicknamed "the Prophet," and the **British** have to do with the **War of 1812**?

_____
_____
_____
_____

8) Clarify the reasons behind America's lack of success when trying to take over land in **Canada** during the **War of 1812**.

_____
_____
_____
_____
_____

9) Evaluate why **Andrew Jackson** was so famous for his role in the **Battle of New Orleans** during the **War of 1812**.

_____
_____
_____
_____
_____
_____

10) Spell out what the **Treaty of Ghent** in 1812 basically accomplished.

_____
_____
_____
_____
_____

11) Who were the biggest losers of the **War of 1812** and why?

_____
_____
_____
_____
_____
_____

12) Why did the **War of 1812** spell the end of the **Federalist Party**?

_____
_____
_____
_____

13) Account for the **nationalist** fervor felt by **Americans** after the **War of 1812** ended.

_____
_____
_____
_____
_____

## The Market Revolution: Crash Course US History #12

1) Go into detail and describe the phenomenon known as the **Market Revolution** (1820s-1850s) in the **United States**.

_____
_____
_____
_____

2) Outline how the **Market Revolution** more closely followed the **Hamiltonian** version of government rather than the **Jeffersonian** version of government.

_____
_____
_____
_____

3) Identify how the **transportation** sector facilitated the **Market Revolution**.

_____
_____
_____
_____

4) Describe how **Robert Fulton's steamboat** changed the **waterways** of America.

_____
_____
_____
_____

5) Analyze what the invention of the **telegraph**, along with quicker access to more information, meant for the **market** sector.

_____
_____

6) How did **factories** in the **United States** contribute to the success of the **Market Revolution** in the **19ᵗʰ Century**?

_____
_____
_____

7) Explain the effects of the **Supreme Court** decision of *Gibbons v. Ogden (1824)*.

_____
_____
_____
_____

8) Point out how the **Market Revolution** in the 19th Century changed the landscape of work.

_____
_____
_____
_____
_____
_____

9) Why did the new concept of working in a **factory,** for a wage under a clock and the whims of an employer, change the idea of American **freedom**?

_____
_____
_____
_____
_____
_____

10) Justify the reasons why a large amount of people migrated west after the **War of 1812**.

_____
_____
_____
_____
_____
_____

11) Explain the 19th century belief of **Manifest Destiny**.

_____
_____
_____
_____
_____
_____

12) What philosophy did the **Transcendentalists** argue and why?

_____
_____
_____

13) Explain how the new **boom and bust cycle** was tied to the formation of **unions**.

_____
_____
_____
_____

14) Why do YOU think the response of **Herman Melville's** character of **Bartleby the Scrivener** saying "I'd rather not work," is both comic and tragic?

_____
_____
_____
_____
_____

## Slavery: Crash Course US History #13

1) Why wouldn't the **North** have been able to **industrialize** as quickly without **Southern cotton**?

_____

_____

_____

_____

2) What were the most prominent effects of the **slave-based economy** in the **South**?

_____

_____

_____

_____

3) Describe a **yeoman** farmer in the **South**.

_____

_____

_____

_____

4) How did **Southern** intellectuals work to encourage white **racial supremacy** in the **South**?

_____

_____

_____

5) Rationalize how **Thomas Jefferson** saw **slavery** as a necessary evil.

_____

_____

_____

_____

_____

6) Evaluate how **masters** could see themselves as benevolent and good even though they supported **slavery**.

_____

_____

_____

_____

7) How did **Americans** in the **Antebellum Era** (1815-1860) justify their insanity over **slavery**?

_____

_____

_____

_____

_____

_____

8) What were conditions like on **plantations** in the **South**?

_____
_____
_____
_____
_____

9) Why did slaves have to be **dehumanized** under the idea of **chattel slavery** in order for **slavery** to function?

_____
_____
_____
_____
_____

10) Justify why YOU think **religion** was an important part of life as a **slave**.

_____
_____
_____
_____
_____
_____

11) Defend why **Harriet Tubman** was considered one of the most famous runaway **slaves**.

_____
_____
_____
_____
_____
_____

12) Illustrate the causes and effects of **Nat Turner's Rebellion** in 1831.

_____
_____
_____
_____
_____
_____

13) How did **slaves** reaffirm their **humanity** even as they were subjected to the harsh conditions of **slavery,** and why is this struggle relevant today?

_____
_____
_____
_____
_____
_____
_____
_____

## Age of Jackson: Crash Course US History #14

1) Go into detail about how the **Market Revolution** caused the **United States Congress** to lower the **property qualifications** needed in order to vote between the years 1820-1850.

_____
_____
_____
_____
_____

2) Describe the **Era of Good Feelings** (1817-1825) during the Presidency of **James Monroe**.

_____
_____
_____

3) Give three examples as to how the **American System** was fueled by **economic nationalism** in the first half of the **19<sup>th</sup> Century**.
   A)_____
   B)_____
   C)_____

4) In a sentence or two, assess the main points of the **Monroe Doctrine**.

_____
_____
_____
_____

5) Why was the **Missouri Compromise** passed by the **United States Congress** in **1820**?

_____
_____
_____
_____

6) Justify the **Election of 1824** and how **John Quincy Adams** became **President of the United States** even though **Andrew Jackson** gained the most **electoral** votes.

_____
_____
_____
_____
_____
_____

7) How did **Andrew Jackson** win the **Election of 1828**?

_____
_____
_____

8) Clarify how the **American Whig Party** emerged as a viable **political party** during **Andrew Jackson's** presidency.

_____

_____

_____

_____

9) What were the consequences of the **Tariff of 1828** and how did this affect **South Carolina**?

_____

_____

_____

_____

_____

10) Explain what happened to the rights of **Native Americans** after the **US Congress** supported the **Indian Removal Act of 1830.**

_____

_____

_____

_____

11) What happened along the **Trail of Tears** in 1838 during **Martin Van Buren's** presidency?

_____

_____

_____

_____

12) Explain the dichotomy (*split in beliefs*) between **Andrew Jackson** and **Nicholas Biddle** over renewing the **charter** of the **Second Bank of the United States**.

_____

_____

_____

_____

13) How did the creation of "**pet banks**" lead to **inflation** and ultimately the **Panic of 1837**?

_____

_____

_____

_____

14) Identify the hallmarks of **Andrew Jackson's** presidency and the irony of his inclusion on the face of the twenty dollar bill.

_____

_____

_____

_____

Name_____

Period_____

Date_____

## 19th Century Reforms: Crash Course US History #15

1) Who were the **Shakers** and how did they separate themselves from the competition?

_____

_____

2) Identify the belief system of the **Mormons**.

_____

_____

3) Explain what was going on inside of the **utopian** experiment at **Brook Farm** and why it was a failure.

_____

_____

_____

4) Evaluate the origins of the **Second Great Awakening** of the 1820s and 1830s.

_____

_____

_____

_____

5) Identify the religious ideology behind the **Second Great Awakening** and how it affected the **Market Revolution**.

_____

_____

_____

_____

6) Analyze what **19ᵗʰ Century reformers** believed in doing.

_____

_____

_____

7) What was the **Temperance Movement** and what did it do?

_____

_____

_____

_____

8) Make clear why the **Temperance Movement** was so controversial.

_____

_____

_____

_____

_____

_____

9) Explain what happened to **education** in the **United States** during the mid-**19th Century**.

_____
_____
_____

10) Illustrate what was going on regarding **abolitionism** and **slavery** during the first third of the **19th Century**.

_____
_____
_____
_____
_____

11) Who was **William Lloyd Garrison** and what was his role as an **abolitionist**?

_____
_____
_____
_____

12) How did **Congress** use the **gag-rule** in 1836 to suppress **free speech** surrounding the issue of **slavery**?

_____
_____
_____
_____

13) Illuminate the reasons why **Frederick Douglass** was so famous.

_____
_____
_____
_____

14) What did **Frederick Douglass** say in front of **Congress** on July 4th, 1852?

_____
_____
_____
_____

15) How did **abolitionists** work towards a more just society, and how did it transform the way that **Americans** saw **slavery**?

_____
_____
_____
_____
_____
_____

## Women in the 19th Century: Crash Course US History #16

1) Analyze the principle of **coverture** and how it pertained to **women** around the time of the **American Revolution**.

_____
_____
_____
_____

2) Describe the attitude American **women** were expected to have according to the ideals of the **Republican Motherhood**.

_____
_____
_____
_____

3) Why were **women** counted in the population if they couldn't vote?

_____
_____
_____
_____

4) How did the **Market Revolution** have an effect on American **women**?

_____
_____
_____
_____

5) Explain the actions of the so-called **Cult of Domesticity**.

_____
_____
_____
_____

6) How did the radical idea of **equality** between men and **women** gain traction in **reform** movements?

_____
_____
_____
_____

7) What exactly was the **Temperance Movement**?

_____
_____
_____
_____
_____

8) Go into detail as to how the **Temperance Movement** made a huge difference in American life during the **19th Century**.

_____
_____
_____
_____
_____
_____

9) Who was **Sarah Grimke**?

_____

10) Why do **Americans** read about and talk about **Harriet Beecher Stowe's <u>Uncle Tom's Cabin</u>** (1852) in United States history classes?

_____
_____
_____
_____
_____

11) Identify one of the arguments used by **pro-slavery** forces against the **equality** for **women**.

_____

12) What happened at the **Seneca Falls Convention of 1848** led by **Elizabeth Cady Stanton** and **Lucretia Mott**?

_____
_____
_____
_____
_____
_____

13) Who was **Sojourner Truth** and how did she advance the rights of **black women**?

_____
_____
_____

14) Clarify why **Amelia Bloomer** became associated with women's fashion.

_____

15) How were the ideals of the **Women's Rights Movement** twisted by critics?

_____
_____
_____

16) Explain how the **Women's Rights Movement** chipped away at the misnomer that a woman's place should be in the home.

_____
_____
_____
_____
_____
_____

Name_____
Period_____
Date_____

## War And Expansion: Crash Course US History #17

1) What did **John L. O'Sullivan** mean when he coined the term **Manifest Destiny**?

_____
_____
_____

2) Explain what was going on in **Oregon** during the first half of the **19<sup>th</sup> Century**.

_____
_____

3) Why did **Mexico** grant a huge tract of land to **Moses Austin**?

_____
_____

4) Explain the causes and effects of the **Battle of the Alamo** in 1836.

_____
_____
_____
_____
_____
_____

5) Why didn't the **United States annex** *(take over without force)* **Texas** in 1837 even though the **Texans** wanted to be part of the **United States**?

_____
_____
_____

6) How did the election of **James K. Polk** to the presidency facilitate the **annexation** of **Texas** in 1845?

_____
_____
_____
_____

7) How did the **Oregon Treaty of 1846** balance the incorporation of **Texas** into the **United States**?

_____
_____
_____
_____
_____
_____

8) Why do YOU think President **Polk** sent future president and **General Zachary Taylor** along with the **US army** to a disputed border in the **South of Texas**?

_____
_____
_____

9) Explain the terms agreed to inside of the **Treaty of Guadalupe Hidalgo of 1848**.

_____
_____
_____
_____
_____

10) Analyze the ideas of **nativism** practiced by the **Know Nothing Party** and how they spread bias against the new **Spanish** and **Mexicans** citizens now living under the jurisdiction of the **United States**.

_____
_____
_____
_____

11) What did the massive influx of **immigrants** during the **California Gold Rush** of 1848-1855 mean for **California**?

_____
_____
_____
_____
_____

12) Interpret the beliefs of the **Free Soil Party** which emerged as a third party in 1848.

_____
_____
_____
_____

13) Outline how **Henry Clay** and the **Compromise of 1850** attempt to solve the issue of **slavery**.
    A)_____
    B)_____
    C)_____
    D)_____

14) Evaluate how the idea of **Manifest Destiny** made the **American Civil War** (1861-1865) inevitable.

_____
_____
_____
_____
_____
_____
_____

Election of 1860: Crash Course US History #18

1) Explain why the **Fugitive Slave Act** was the most controversial part of the **Compromise of 1850**.

_____
_____
_____
_____
_____
_____
_____

2) What was the problem with **Steven Douglass' Transcontinental Railroad**?

_____
_____
_____
_____
_____
_____
_____
_____
_____
_____

3) Evaluate the importance of the **Kansas-Nebraska Act of 1854**, which included **popular sovereignty**, in determining its **slavery** issue. Include how it related to the **Missouri Compromise of 1820**.

_____
_____
_____
_____
_____
_____
_____
_____
_____
_____
_____
_____

4) How and why did the **Republican Party** form in the **1850s**?

_____
_____
_____
_____
_____
_____

5) Analyze the conspiracy theory many **abolitionists** saw in the passage of the **Kansas-Nebraska Act of 1854** by the **United States Congress**.

_____
_____
_____
_____
_____
_____
_____
_____
_____

6) Explain what happened in the aftermath of **Chief Justice Roger B. Taney's Supreme Court** decision of *Dred Scott v. Sanford (1857)*.

_____
_____
_____
_____
_____
_____
_____
_____
_____
_____
_____
_____
_____
_____

7) Who was **John Brown** and what did he plan to do once he captured **Harper's Ferry**?

_____
_____
_____
_____
_____
_____
_____

8) After **Republican Abraham Lincoln** won the **Election of 1860**, what was the immediate decision of the **Southern States**?

_____
_____
_____
_____
_____
_____
_____
_____
_____
_____

Battles of the Civil War: Crash Course US History #19

1) In 1861, the first shots of the **American Civil War** were fired at
_____ in _____.

2) Who won the **American Civil War**? The **Northern Union Army** or the **Southern Confederate Army**?

_____

_____

3) Where did the **Battle of the First Bull Run** in 1861 take place and who won?

_____

_____

_____

4) In 1862, what was the initial battle won by the **North**?

_____

_____

_____

5) Name a few battles fought in the **West** by the **Northern Union Army** and the **Southern Confederate Army**.

_____

_____

_____

_____

6) For the first time, two ironclad warships the **USS Monitor** and the **CSS Virginia** fought along the **Mississippi River** in this battle won by whom?

_____

_____

_____

7) What battles did the **United States** win that gave the Union the **Port of New Orleans**?

_____

_____

8) What do YOU think the significance of capturing the **Port of New Orleans** in 1862 from the **South** had on the outcome of the **American Civil War**?

_____

_____

_____

_____

_____

9) The **Seven Days Battles** between **Confederate General Robert E. Lee** and **Union General George McClellan** where fought in which state resulting in what?

_____

_____

_____

10) Late in the **Summer of 1862**, list all the battles won by the **Confederate Army**.

_____

_____

11) Explain what happened in the **Battle of Antietam** in 1862 and why it was such an important battle in the **American Civil War**.

_____

_____

_____

_____

12) What happened to **General Stonewall Jackson** of the **Confederate Army** at the **Battle of Chancellorsville** in May of 1863?

_____

_____

_____

_____

13) What did the **Battle of Vicksburg** in 1863 effectively do in favor of the **Union Army**?

_____

_____

_____

_____

14) Why was the **Battle of Gettysburg** in 1863 considered one of the most important battles of the **American Civil War**? (Include **Pickett's Charge** and **Lincoln's Gettysburg Address** in your answer)

_____

_____

_____

_____

15) In which **American Civil War** battle did **US President Abraham Lincoln** almost get shot?

_____

_____

16) Name a few of the **Battles of 1864** and who won them.

_____

_____

_____

_____

17) What happened at the decisive battle at the **Appomattox Courthouse** in **Virginia** on **April 8, 1865** and what was the result?

_____

_____

_____

_____

_____

The Civil War, Part 1: Crash Course US History #20

1) Why do YOU think the border **slave** states of **Maryland**, **Missouri**, **Tennessee**, and **West Virginia** did not join the **Confederacy**, yet participated on the **Union side** and allowed **slavery** in their states for the majority of the **American Civil War**?

_____
_____
_____
_____
_____
_____

2) Why were these non-participatory states important to the **Union**?

_____
_____
_____

3) Who fought against whom in the **American Civil War** and why?

_____
_____
_____
_____
_____

4) Analyze the **Nullification Crisis of the 1830s** and how the **Virginia and Kentucky Resolutions of 1798-1799** supported this behavior.

_____
_____
_____
_____
_____
_____
_____

5) What were the first items on the agenda that the newly formed **Confederate** government passed in order to ensure their survival as a country?

_____
_____
_____
_____

6) Outline the advantages that the **Union Army** had over the **Confederate Army** in the **American Civil War**.

_____
_____
_____
_____
_____
_____

7) How did the **railroads** help the **North** to win the **American Civil War** over the **South**?

_____

_____

_____

8) Identify the only **military advantage** that the **South** had during the **Civil War**.

_____

_____

9) What was wrong with the **war of attrition** theory that some have argued that the **South** needed to do to win the **Civil War**?

_____

_____

_____

_____

_____

10) How was **Union General Ulysses S. Grant** different from other **Union** generals?

_____

_____

_____

11) Why did the war to end **slavery** have very little appeal for many **Northerners** fighting for the **Union**?

_____

_____

_____

_____

12) What did **Southerners** find that motivated them to fight for the **Confederacy**?

_____

_____

_____

_____

13) If **Confederate General Robert E. Lee** had won the **Battle of Gettysburg**, what would have happened to the **Northern** war effort?

_____

_____

_____

14) Why was **Union General Sherman's** taking of **Atlanta** seen as a crushing blow to the **Confederacy**?

_____

_____

_____

_____

_____

## The Civil War, Part 2: Crash Course US History #21

1) Explain how the **Emancipation Proclamation** executive order by **Abraham Lincoln** didn't actually free all the slaves in spite of taking effect on **January 1, 1963**.

_____
_____
_____
_____
_____

2) Why didn't **Abraham Lincoln** free the **slaves** in the **border states** that remained loyal to the **Union**?

_____
_____
_____
_____
_____

3) In what way was **Abraham Lincoln** essentially forced to issue the **Emancipation Proclamation**?

_____
_____
_____
_____
_____

4) How did the threat of the **British** joining the **Confederacy** factor into **Abraham Lincoln's** decision to issue the **Emancipation Proclamation**?

_____
_____
_____
_____
_____
_____

5) Contemplate **Abraham Lincoln's** viewpoint In the **Gettysburg Address**. Why did he consider the **American Civil War** a second **American Revolution**?

_____
_____
_____
_____
_____
_____
_____

6) Who was **Matthew Brady** and what was his role in the **American Civil War**?

_____
_____
_____
_____
_____
_____

7) What did the **Northern victory** in the **American Civil War** mean for the **United States**?

_____
_____
_____
_____
_____

8) Why is **Abraham Lincoln** considered by many to be the first American president to expand the power of the **executive** office?

_____
_____
_____
_____
_____

9) By what means did the **Homestead Act of 1862**, passed by the **Republican** controlled **Congress**, play a role in the **Federalization** of the **United States**?

_____
_____
_____
_____
_____

10) After what precedent did the **Pacific Railway Act of 1862** effectively tie the nation together?

_____
_____
_____
_____
_____

11) Analyze the origin of **greenbacks** and what factors led to their existence.

_____
_____
_____
_____

12) Point out why the **American Civil War** was ultimately a victory for **Federalist Alexander Hamilton's** vision of what the **United States** should be?

_____
_____
_____
_____
_____

Name_____
Period_____
Date_____

## Reconstruction and 1876: Crash Course US History #22

1) Explain what the **Freedman's Bureau** did to change the lives for the former **slaves** during the 1860s.

_____
_____
_____
_____
_____

2) How did the system of **sharecropping** work in the **Southern United States**?

_____
_____
_____
_____
_____

3) Why was the system of **sharecropping** problematic for both poor **white farmers** and the newly freed **black farmers**?

_____
_____
_____
_____
_____

4) How did the **Civil Rights Bill of 1866,** passed by **Radical Republicans** in the **House**, re-define the concept of **citizenship** in the **United States**?

_____
_____
_____
_____

5) Spell out how the **United States Congress** responded to **President Andrew Johnson's** veto of the **Civil Rights Bill of 1866**.

_____
_____
_____
_____

6) What was **14th Amendment** and how did it change the rights of **African-Americans**?

_____
_____
_____
_____
_____
_____
_____
_____

7) Analyze the effects of the **Reconstruction Act of 1867**.

_____
_____
_____
_____
_____
_____
_____
_____
_____
_____

8) Analyze the effects of the **15<sup>th</sup> Amendment** to the **Constitution**.

_____
_____
_____
_____
_____
_____
_____
_____
_____

9) How did the **Federal Government** come to be seen as the custodian of freedom?

_____
_____
_____
_____

10) Give reasons as to why the **Period of Reconstruction** (1865-1877) ended.

_____
_____
_____
_____
_____
_____

11) How did the **Economic Depression of 1873** lead to **Corrupt Bargain of 1877** which in effect ended the **Period of Reconstruction** (1865-1877)?

_____
_____
_____
_____
_____
_____
_____

12) Identify a lesser known failure of the **Period of Reconstruction** (1865-1877).

_____
_____
_____
_____
_____
_____
_____
_____

## The Industrial Economy: Crash Course US History #23

1) How did the **geography** of the **United States** make it ripe for an **industrial boom** in the second half of the **19th Century**?

_____
_____
_____
_____

2) Analyze the **demography** of the **United States** and show how **immigrants** added to the **industrial boom** in the second half of the **19th Century**.

_____
_____
_____
_____
_____
_____

3) Explain how **railroads** were one of the keys to the **Second Industrial Revolution's** (1870-1914) success.

_____
_____
_____
_____
_____

4) Connect how **railroads** could be considered the first modern **corporations**.

_____
_____
_____
_____
_____
_____

5) Assess how the **Captains of Industry** could also be considered as **Robber Barons**.

_____
_____
_____
_____
_____
_____
_____

injuries
prior pay
depression

6) Explain the differences between **vertical integration** and **horizontal integration** inside of **corporate structure**.

_____
_____
_____
_____
_____

7) Apply concepts to show how there was job insecurity due to **immigration** in the late **19ᵗʰ Century**.

_____
_____
_____

8) Show how the **Knights of Labor union**, led by **Terrance Powderly**, was irreparably damaged by the **Haymarket Riot** in 1886.

_____
_____
_____
_____

9) Show how the union, the **American Federation of Labor (AFL)** under **Samuel Gompers**, was different than the **Knights of Labor**.

_____
_____
_____
_____
_____

10) Critique how the pseudoscience of **Social Darwinism** was used to argue that some people were better than others?

_____
_____
_____
_____

11) What social, political, and economic factors led to violent strikes such as the **Homestead Strike** in 1892 and the **Pullman Strike** in 1894?

_____
_____
_____
_____
_____
_____

Westward Expansion: Crash Course US History #24

1) Identify what the **Western Native Americans** were forced to do as a result of the **Westward Expansion** of the **United States**.

_____

_____

_____

2) Explain what happened to **Mexicans** at the end of the **Mexican-American War** (1846-1848) who were living in the area affected by the **Treaty of Guadalupe-Hidalgo** (1848).

_____

_____

_____

3) Illuminate how the invention of the **railroad** enabled Americans in the **United States** to migrate west.

_____

_____

_____

_____

4) Describe the existence of **Plains Tribes** and include what ultimately happened to them in the **19ᵗʰ Century**.

_____

_____

_____

5) Justify the origins of the **Native American** ritual of the **Ghost Dance** that spread as a result of resistance to **US** removal policies.

_____

_____

_____

_____

6) Clarify the reasons behind the **Battle of Little Big Horn** (1876), aka **Custer's Last Stand**, including the end result.

_____

_____

_____

_____

_____

_____

_____

7) How did the **US Government** deal with the **land** held by **Native Americans** during the latter half of the **19<sup>th</sup> Century**?

_____
_____
_____
_____
_____
_____

8) What was the purpose of the most famous boarding school responsible for the civilizing of **Native** people?

_____
_____
_____
_____

9) Identify the nature of the **Cowboys** and include how their support of the **beef industry** was tied to their practice.

_____
_____
_____
_____
_____
_____

10) How did farming in the **West** quickly go from small family farms to those owned by the banks?

_____
_____
_____
_____
_____
_____

11) Explain how the **Oregon Trail** and the **Wild West** are related.

_____
_____
_____
_____
_____
_____
_____
_____
_____

## Growth, Cities, and Immigration: Crash Course US History #25

1) Identify the effects of the passage of the **Homestead Act of 1862**.

_____
_____
_____
_____
_____

2) What is the difference between the terms **rural** and **urban**?

_____
_____
_____
_____

3) What made the growth of **cities** possible between the years 1880-1920?

_____
_____
_____
_____

4) Point out how some **inventions** during the **Gilded Age** (1865-1896) were so revolutionary.

_____
_____
_____
_____
_____

5) How did **New York City** lead the way during this time of **immigration influx** in the **United States**?

_____
_____
_____
_____
_____

6) Who were the **Irish** and what did many do once they got to the **United States**?

_____
_____
_____
_____

7) Identify what the **German immigrants** mainly did when they came to the **United States**.

_____
_____
_____
_____
_____

8) By the 1890s, why did so many **Southern and Eastern European immigrants** flood into the **United States**?

_____
_____
_____
_____
_____
_____

9) Why were **Chinese immigrants** discriminated against during the **Gilded Age** (1865-1896)?

_____
_____
_____
_____
_____
_____

10) Analyze how the new **transportation technology** of the **Gilded Age** (1865-1896) allowed people to get around.

_____
_____
_____
_____
_____
_____

11) What were the most notable features of **Gilded Age** (1865-1896) **cities** such as **New York**?

_____
_____
_____
_____
_____
_____

12) How is the America we live in **today** shaped by the influx of **immigrants** of the **19th Century**?

_____
_____
_____
_____
_____
_____
_____

Gilded Age Politics: Crash Course US History #26

1) How did **William "Boss" Tweed's** feat of swindling the public with **kickbacks** explain how the **urban political machine** worked during the **Gilded Age** (1865-1896)?

_____
_____
_____
_____
_____
_____
_____

2) Elaborate how **Tammany Hall politicians** could always fall back upon fraud in order to get votes during the **Gilded Age** (1865-1896).

_____
_____
_____
_____
_____
_____

3) Describe the ideology **Gilded Age Republican politicians** favored for their parties.

_____
_____
_____
_____

4) Describe the ideology **Gilded Age Democrat politicians** favored for their parties.

_____
_____
_____
_____

5) Point out the main similarity between the two **political parties** of the **Democrats** and **Republicans** during the **Gilded Age** (1865-1896).

_____
_____
_____
_____
_____

6) What was the unintended effect of the **Civil Service Act of 1883**?

_____
_____
_____
_____
_____

7) Outline how the **Sherman Anti-Trust Act of 1890** was a failure.

_____

_____

8) How were **Jim Crow Laws** biased against **African Americans**?

_____

_____

_____

_____

_____

9) Why was the **Grange Movement** formed by **farmers** in the **1870s**?

_____

_____

10) Explain the advantages the **Grange Movement** created for the **Farmers Alliance**.

_____

_____

_____

_____

_____

11) List a few of the reforms that the **People's Party,** aka the **Populists,** achieved.

_____

_____

_____

_____

12) Spell out the **demographic** that added to the voting power of the **Populists** in the **1890s**.

_____

_____

13) Rationalize the problem of the **Populists Party** platform around the **free coinage** of **silver**.

_____

_____

_____

14) Give reasons why **Democratic** nominee **William Jennings Bryan** was the best-known **Populist candidate** in the **Election of 1896**.

_____

_____

_____

_____

_____

## The Progressive Era: Crash Course US History #27

1) Briefly spell out the hallmarks of the **Progressive Era** (1890-1920).

_____
_____
_____

2) Identify the problem **companies** and **corporations** had in order to make profits. (Include how they solved this dilemma.)

_____
_____
_____
_____

3) Define the term **muckraking** in regards to the magazines of the **Progressive Era** (1890-1920).

_____
_____
_____
_____
_____

4) Explain how the central theme of the novel **The Jungle** (1906) by **Upton Sinclair** could be seen as **progressive muckraking**.

_____
_____
_____
_____
_____

5) Why did workers organize into **unions** during the **Progressive Era** (1890-1920)?

_____
_____
_____

6) Expound upon the origins of the **Industrial Workers of the World; aka the Wobblies.**

_____
_____
_____

7) Outline the philosophy of the **Wobblies**.

_____
_____
_____

8) Clarify what is meant by the birth of a **mass consumption society**.

_____
_____
_____
_____

9) What were most **Progressives** concerned about in regards to **industrial capitalism**?

_____
_____
_____
_____

10) Why do YOU think a **progressive** agenda was more popular at the local level, especially in the cities, rather than at the **national** level?

_____
_____
_____

11) The **17ᵗʰ Amendment** allowed for what aspects of **direct democracy**?

_____
_____
_____

12) How did **Progressives** limit **immigrant** participation in **direct democracy**?

_____
_____
_____
_____

13) Clarify how **Jim Crow Laws** limited **direct democracy** in the **Southern States**.

_____
_____
_____
_____

14) Explain how the **Supreme Court** decision in *Plessy v. Ferguson (1896)* upheld **Jim Crow Laws** and limited **civil rights** for **African Americans**.

_____
_____
_____
_____
_____
_____
_____

15) Explain why not all **African Americans** shared **Booker T. Washington's** inclusive stance to the new **separate but equal** laws.

_____
_____
_____
_____
_____
_____

16) How were the agendas of the **Progressives** similar to what many activists do today?

_____
_____
_____
_____
_____
_____

## American Imperialism: Crash Course US History #28

1) Explain how **economics** was one of the primary causes of **American imperialism**.

_____
_____
_____
_____
_____

2) Outline the social, political, and economic repercussions of the **Panic of 1893**.

_____
_____
_____
_____
_____
_____
_____

3) Explain what **Captain Alfred Thayer Mahan** argued in his book, **The Influence of Sea Power Upon History** (1890).

_____
_____
_____

4) Why do YOU think Americans began to say the **Pledge of Allegiance** en masse during the 1890s?

_____
_____
_____
_____
_____
_____

5) Describe how the **United States** annexed **Hawaii** in 1898.

_____
_____
_____

6) Briefly outline the causes of the **War of 1898 (Spanish-American War)** between the **United States** and **Spain**.

_____
_____
_____
_____
_____
_____
_____

7) How did the **War of 1898** launch the political career of **Theodore (Teddy) Roosevelt**?

_____

_____

_____

_____

8) Territories acquired from **Spain** as a result of the **War of 1898** include:

a) _____ b) _____ c) _____

9) Reveal what the **Platt Amendment** to the **Cuban Constitution** authorized the **United States** military to do.

_____

_____

_____

10) Why do YOU think atrocities by **American** soldiers against the **Filipinos** helped to create the **Anti-Imperialist League**, which included **Mark Twain**?

_____

_____

_____

_____

11) Explain how **Puerto Rico** is a **territory** owned by the **United States**.

_____

_____

_____

_____

12) Rationalize why was the island of **Hawaii** was treated differently than **Puerto Rico** and the **Philippines**.

_____

_____

_____

_____

_____

_____

13) What did **United States Senator Albert Beveridge** argue in support of **imperialism**?

_____

_____

_____

_____

_____

14) In the end, what was the ideology of **imperialism** driven by and why?

_____

_____

_____

_____

_____

## The Progressive Presidents: Crash Course US History #29

1) Why has **Theodore (Teddy) Roosevelt** been considered a model **20th Century** president?

_____

_____

_____

_____

2) Describe what **Theodore Roosevelt's Square Deal** set out to accomplish.

_____

_____

_____

3) How did **Theodore Roosevelt** become known as a **trust-buster** in respect to his usage of the **Sherman Anti-Trust Act of 1890**?

_____

_____

_____

_____

_____

_____

4) Demonstrate what the **Hepburn Act of 1906** accomplished.

_____

_____

_____

_____

5) How was **Theodore Roosevelt** a **conservationist** (a protector of the environment)?

_____

_____

_____

_____

6) What platform did **socialist** and presidential candidate **Eugene Debs** run on?

_____

_____

_____

_____

7) Explain US President **Woodrow Wilson's New Freedom** program.

_____

_____

_____

_____

_____

_____

_____

_____

8) What did **Theodore Roosevelt's Bull Moose Party** platform during the **Election of 1912** call for?

_____

_____

9) In **President Woodrow Wilson's New Freedom** program, what did the **Underwood Tariff of 1913 (Revenue Act of 1913)** accomplish?

_____

_____

10) What did the **16ᵗʰ Amendment** make into law?

_____

11) How did the creation of the **Federal Reserve System** in 1913 expand the power of the national government?

_____

_____

12) What does **Theodore Roosevelt's** motto, "Speak softly and carry a big stick," actually mean?

_____

_____

_____

13) Explain why YOU think the **United States** wanted control of the **Panama Canal**.

_____

_____

_____

_____

14) How did the **Roosevelt Corollary** amplify the **Monroe Doctrine**?

_____

_____

_____

15) Explain **President William H. Taft's** policy of **Dollar Diplomacy**.

_____

_____

_____

16) Analyze what happened during the American **military** intervention in **Veracruz, Mexico**.

_____

_____

17) Why was this period of **Progressive politics** in American History important?

_____

_____

_____

_____

_____

_____

## America in World War I: Crash Course US History #30

1) Even though **World War I** (1914-1918) broke out in **Europe** in 1914, why was the initial policy of the **United States** to remain **neutral**?

_____

_____

_____

2) Analyze the slogan **President Woodrow Wilson** used to court the **Progressives** who were against the **United States** entering **World War I** during the **Election of 1916**.

_____

_____

3) Why didn't the **United States** immediately go to war after the sinking of the **Lusitania**, a **British** ocean liner en route to **New York**, by **German submarines** in 1915?

_____

_____

4) Outline three other possible reasons why the **United States** declared war against **Germany** on April 2, 1917.

_____

_____

_____

_____

_____

_____

5) Briefly explain how the **United States** helped out the **Entente Powers** economically in **World War I** (1914-1918).

_____

6) How did the addition of 1,000,000 **American** troops deployed in 1917 help the **Entente Powers** defeat the **Central Powers** and the **German Army**?

_____

_____

_____

7) Describe the economic factors which allowed the **United States** to emerge more powerful after the end of **World War I** (1914-1918).

1) Selective service

2) combat economy

3) repurpose industry

4) agriculture

5) transportation

8) How did the regulations by the **United States** control the **economy** during wartime and ultimately bring about the goals laid out by the **Progressives Party**?

_____
_____
_____

9) Illuminate how the **United States** actively shaped public opinion during **World War I** (1914-1918).

_____
_____
_____
_____

10) Justify why **civil liberties** in the **United States** were repressed during **World War I** (1914-1918).

_____
_____
_____
_____

11) Describe the **Sedition Act of 1917**.

_____
_____
_____
_____

12) In the **Supreme Court Case** *Schenck v. the United States (1919)*, what was the ultimate decision?

_____
_____
_____
_____
_____

13) Explain what happened during the **Palmer Raids** soon after the end of **World War I**.

_____
_____
_____
_____

14) Why wasn't **Woodrow Wilson's** dream of a **League of Nations** realized at the end of **World War I**?

_____
_____
_____
_____
_____
_____

Women's Suffrage: Crash Course US History #31

1) Define the legal changes **women** faced during the **Progressive Era** (1890-1920).

_____
_____
_____
_____
_____
_____

2) Explain how **women** influenced the **Christian Temperance Union** under **Frances Willard**.

_____
_____
_____
_____

3) What did the **National Consumers League** hope to achieve by sponsoring **boycotts**?

_____
_____
_____

4) Explain what having a job outside of the household did for **women**.

_____
_____
_____

5) Evaluate what **Charlotte Perkins Gilman** was trying to achieve in her book, **Women and Economics** (1898).

_____
_____
_____

6) Why do YOU think **Emma Goldman** was arrested over 40 times for talking about **women** sharing ideas about **female sexuality** and **birth control** in the **1920s**?

_____
_____
_____

7) Explain how **Jane Addams' Hull House** in **Chicago** helped female **European immigrants** during the **Progressive Age** (1890-1920).

_____
_____
_____
_____
_____

8) What did many states do before **women** were officially granted the right to vote with the passage of the **19th Amendment** in 1919?

_____
_____
_____
_____
_____
_____

9) Analyze the **suffrage movement** culminating in the **19th Amendment** giving **women** the right to vote.

_____
_____
_____
_____
_____
_____
_____
_____
_____

10) Defend US President **Woodrow Wilson's** feelings about **women's suffrage**.

_____
_____
_____
_____

11) Rationalize how granting **women** the right to vote after the passage of the **19th Amendment** could be seen as anti-climactic.

_____
_____
_____
_____
_____

12) In a nutshell, what were **Alice Paul's** beliefs?

_____
_____
_____
_____

13) Even with the passage of the **19th Amendment**, why do YOU think there still wasn't an immediate change in the roles **women** were expected to play?

_____
_____
_____
_____
_____
_____
_____
_____

The Roaring 20s: Crash Course US History #32

1) What did American presidents do in the **1920s** that was a change from the presidents of the **Progressive Era** (1890-1920)?

_____
_____
_____
_____
_____
_____

2) Analyze how **productivity** rose dramatically in the **1920s**.

_____
_____
_____
_____
_____
_____

3) Describe a couple of **labor savings** devices that **consumers** purchased in the **1920s**.

_____
_____
_____
_____

4) How did **Swing Dancing** and the **Charleston** change the nature of dance?

_____
_____
_____
_____
_____

5) Identify **Charles Lindbergh's** claim to fame.

_____
_____
_____

6) Why did writer **Gertrude Stein** call her fellow writers a "**Lost Generation**?"

_____
_____
_____
_____
_____

7) Evaluate how the **Harlem Renaissance** added to the culture of **African Americans**.

_____
_____
_____
_____
_____
_____

8) What was different about the social culture of young **Western women,** known as **Flappers**, and how did these girls change the social culture of the **United States**?

_____
_____
_____
_____
_____
_____

9) Explain how the **First Amendment** was upheld in the **Supreme Court** case *Near vs. Minnesota (1931)*.

_____
_____
_____
_____
_____
_____

10) Identify the groups that the **Ku Klux Klan** denounced in the **1920s**.

_____
_____
_____

11) Analyze the **Immigration Act of 1924** signed into law by **President Calvin Coolidge**.

_____
_____
_____
_____

12) Rationalize why the **Scopes Trial of 1925** was a victory for science.

_____
_____
_____
_____
_____

## The Great Depression: Crash Course US History #33

1) Point out how the **credit boom**, **mass consumption**, and the lavish **economic spending** of the **1920s** ultimately led to the **Stock Market Crash of 1929**.

_____
_____
_____
_____
_____

2) Describe the factors that made the US **economy** ripe for a **Great Depression**.

_____
_____
_____
_____
_____

3) Briefly describe what the term "**margin buying**" actually means.

_____
_____
_____

4) Rationalize what the **Federal Reserve System**, created in 1913, did for the **United States**.

_____
_____
_____

5) Why didn't creating a **Federal Reserve System** work to solve the banking crisis of the **1930s**?

_____
_____
_____
_____

6) Describe why **deflation** is worse than **inflation**.

_____
_____
_____
_____
_____
_____
_____

7) How did **Germany** pay for its **war debts** under the **Treaty of Versailles**?

_____
_____
_____
_____
_____
_____
_____

8) Account for the **Stock Market Crash of 1929** and analyze how this contributed to the **Great Depression** (1929-1939) in the **1930s**.

_____
_____
_____
_____
_____
_____
_____

9) Explain how the **protectionist** trade policies of the **Hawley-Smoot Tariff Bill of 1930** not only **raised tax** levels but also sunk the **United States** deeper into a **depression**.

_____
_____
_____
_____
_____
_____
_____

10) Outline the reasons why so many **banks** failed by 1931.

_____
_____
_____
_____
_____

11) What did **President Hoover** believe the best course of action was for the government to combat the **Great Depression** (1929-1939)?

_____
_____
_____
_____

12) Briefly explain the solution that finally helped to end the ongoing financial crisis of the **Great Depression** (1929-1939) inside of the **United States**.

_____
_____
_____
_____
_____
_____
_____

## FDR and the New Deal: Crash Course US History #34

1) Explain the solution proposed by **United States President Franklin D Roosevelt** (FDR) for the ending of the **Great Depression** (1929-1939)?

_____
_____
_____
_____

2) What is meant by the "relief" part of the **New Deal**?

_rel_____
_____
_____

3) What is meant by the "recovery," part of the **New Deal**?

_____
_____
_____

4) What is meant by the "reform," part of the **New Deal**?

_____
_____

5) Name a few of the **New Deal** programs and how they helped to expand **socialism** in the United States.

_____
_____
_____
_____

6) What is the **FDIC** and what does it do?

_____
_____
_____
_____

7) What motivates the normally "gridlocked" **Congress** to pass lots of legislative reforms?

_____
_____
_____
_____
_____
_____
_____
_____

8) What was the role of the **Federal Emergency Relief Administration**?

_____
_____
_____

9) What did the **Tennessee River Valley Authority** do that was so controversial?

_____
_____
_____
_____
_____
_____

10) Why was the **Agricultural Adjustment Act (AAA)** so contentious?

_____
_____
_____
_____

11) Explain how the **Dustbowl** from the **drought** in the **Midwest** affected the **United States** in the **1930s**.

_____
_____
_____
_____

12) Briefly analyze the focus of the **Second New Deal**.

_____
_____
_____

13) What did the **Wagner Act of 1935 (National Labor Relations Act)** guarantee to workers?

_____
_____
_____
_____

14) Analyze the benefits of the **Social Security Act of 1935.**

_____
_____
_____
_____

15) Briefly explain the **Works Progress Administration (WPA)**.

_____
_____
_____
_____

16) Do YOU think the **New Deal** was successful?  Explain why or why not.

_____
_____
_____
_____

World War II Part 1: Crash Course US History #35

1) Clarify **United States foreign policy** at the outbreak of **World War II** (1939-1945).

_____
_____
_____
_____

2) Analyze the **Good Neighbor** policy the **United States** had with **Latin America**.

_____
_____
_____
_____
_____

3) Outline the **isolationist** policies of the **United States** during the outset of **World War II** (1939-1945).

_____
_____
_____
_____

4) Explain the idea of **neutrality** behind the **Cash and Carry** policy of the **United States** and how it was biased towards the **Allies** rather than the **Axis** powers.

_____
_____
_____

5) What was the purpose of the **Lend-Lease Act of 1941**, and how did it benefit the countries who were recipients of this act?

_____
_____
_____
_____
_____

6) Outline how the attack by the **Japanese** at **Pearl Harbor** on **December 7, 1941** pushed the **United States** to declare war not only with **Japan** but also with **Germany**.

_____
_____
_____
_____
_____

7) How did the strategy of **island hopping** help the **United States** to win the **Battle of the Pacific** during **World War II** (1939-1945)?

_____
_____
_____
_____
_____

8) Why wasn't **Joseph Stalin** of the **USSR (Soviet Union** aka **Russia)** happy with the **Allies** during **World War II** (1939-1945)?

_____
_____
_____
_____
_____
_____
_____

9) Justify why **Japan** surrendered unconditionally to the **Allies** during **World War II** (1939-1945).

_____
_____
_____
_____
_____

10) Analyze whether the use of **atomic bombs** by the United States during **World War II** (1939-1945) was justified or unethical.

_____
_____
_____
_____
_____
_____

11) Why do YOU think is it important to think about **US President Harry S. Truman's** decision to drop the **atomic bomb**?

_____
_____
_____
_____
_____
_____
_____
_____
_____
_____

World War II Homefront: Crash Course US History #36

1) Evaluate how **World War II** (1939-1945) both strengthened and weakened the **Federal Government**.

_____
_____
_____
_____
_____
_____

2) What was the **population** inside of the **United States** forced to do as a result of commencement of **World War II** (1939-1945)?

_____
_____
_____
_____
_____

3) How did **big business** become even bigger during **World War II** (1939-1945)?

_____
_____
_____
_____

4) Analyze the **demographic** changes inside of **US factories**.

_____
_____
_____
_____

5) Briefly describe **Franklin Delano Roosevelt's (FDR)** new **economic rights** package.

_____
_____
_____
_____
_____

6) Outline the reasons for the **GI Bill of Rights**.

_____
_____
_____
_____
_____

7) Analyze **antisemitism** in the **United States** and what that meant for **Jewish** people suffering at the hands of the **Nazis** in **Europe**.

_____
_____
_____
_____
_____

8) Explain the **social** causes and effects of the **Zoot Suit Riots**.

_____
_____
_____
_____
_____

9) Reveal the reasons for **Executive Order 9066** and how it affected **Japanese-Americans.**

_____
_____
_____

10) Do you think it was **morally** justified to put **Japanese-Americans** into **internment camps** in order to "protect" **American** interests? Why or why not? Defend your answer.

_____
_____
_____
_____
_____
_____
_____
_____
_____

11) Why was the **world bank** created?

_____
_____
_____

12) Briefly outline the goals of the newly formed **United Nations** in 1944.

_____
_____
_____

13) What did **World War II** (1939-1945) do for the **United States economy**?

_____
_____
_____
_____
_____
_____

## The Cold War Era: Crash Course US History #37

1) Why is it best to think of the **Cold War** (1945-1991) as an era?

_____
_____
_____
_____

2) Describe why the **United States** and the **USSR (Soviet Union)** were the only two countries left with any power after **World War II** (1939-1945).

_____
_____
_____
_____
_____
_____

3) Explain why the **United States** countered the **Soviets** with a **Policy of Containment**.

_____
_____
_____
_____
_____

4) Rationalize why the **United States** has been interested in the **Middle East** since **World War II** (1939-1945).

_____
_____
_____
_____

5) Paraphrase the **Truman Doctrine**. What did it say?

_____
_____
_____
_____

6) Clarify the reasons why the United States gave **economic** assistance to **European economies** at the end of **World War II** (1939-1945) under the **Marshall Plan**.

_____
_____
_____
_____
_____

7) Illustrate what was going on in **West Berlin** during the **Berlin Air Lift** (1949) and state the immediate repercussions.

_____
_____
_____

8) How did the **U.S.** lawmakers unify and cast the **Cold War** (1945-1991) to **Americans**?

_____
_____
_____

9) What was the goal of the **American** interventions in **Europe** and in **Asia**?

_____
_____
_____
_____
_____

10) Why did the **U.S. Congress** add the term, "under God," to the **Pledge of Allegiance** in 1954?

_____
_____
_____
_____

11) Rationalize how the obsessive fear with **Communism** started in the **United States**.

_____
_____
_____

12) Explain how the "**Red Scare**," and **Senator Joseph McCarthy** are related.

_____
_____
_____
_____
_____
_____

13) How did the **Cold War** (1945-1991) change the definition of **freedom** for **Americans**?

_____
_____
_____
_____
_____
_____
_____

Name_____
Period_____
Date_____

Cold War Asia: Crash Course US History #38

1) When and where did the **Cold War** (1947-1991) between the **United States** and the **USSR (Union of Soviet Socialist Republics)** really heat up?

_____
_____
_____
_____
_____

2) Evaluate why the **Korean War** (1950-1953) is sometimes called the forgotten war.

_____
_____
_____
_____
_____

3) Clarify how the **Korean War** (1950-1953) helped to elect General **Dwight D. Eisenhower** to the **US Presidency**.

_____
_____
_____
_____
_____

4) By what means did the **Korean War** (1950-1953) help to strengthen the mentality of the **Cold War** (1947-1991)?

_____
_____
_____
_____
_____

5) What factors led to the reasons why **North Vietnamese** leader **Ho Chi Minh** fought against the **United States** in the **Vietnam War** (1955-1975)?

_____
_____
_____
_____
_____

6) Why did the **United States** think it was important to keep **Vietnam** from becoming **communist**?

_____
_____
_____

7) Explain the causes behind the escalation of the **Vietnam War** (1955-1975).

_____
_____
_____
_____
_____
_____
_____

8) Why do YOU think many historians blame the escalation of the **Vietnam War** (1955-1975) on **President Lyndon B. Johnson** even though multiple US presidents ordered **American** troops to **Vietnam**?

_____
_____
_____
_____
_____
_____

9) How did the **Tet Offensive** (1968), by the **North Vietnamese** forces **(Vietcong)**, prolong the outcome of the **Vietnam War** (1955-1975)?

_____
_____
_____
_____
_____
_____

10) How did **Richard Nixon** appeal to **Americans** in the **Election of 1968** in order to help him win the US presidency?

_____
_____
_____
_____
_____
_____

11) Analyze the response of the **US Congress** to the release of the **Pentagon Papers** in 1971.

_____
_____
_____
_____
_____
_____
_____

12) Outline the conditions of the **Paris Peace Accords of 1973** that officially ended the **Vietnam War** (1955-1975).

_____
_____
_____
_____
_____
_____

Civil Rights and the 1950s: Crash Course US History #39

1) Clarify why the **1950s** were a period of prosperity in the **United States**.

_____
_____
_____
_____
_____

2) Identify the items the new **middle class** of **Americans** now had access to in the **1950s**.

_____
_____
_____
_____
_____

3) Explain why the **1950s** were considered an era of **suburbanization**.

_____
_____
_____
_____
_____

4) Interpret how the new **car culture** changed the way **Americans** lived and shopped.

_____
_____
_____
_____
_____

5) Illustrate the **American values** that most **Americans** agreed upon in the **1950s**.

_____
_____
_____
_____
_____

6) Rationalize why the **1950s** weren't a period of expanding opportunities for **African Americans** or people of **color**.

_____
_____
_____
_____

7) Paraphrase the ruling of the **California Supreme Court** case of *Mendez v. Westminster (1947)*.

_____
_____
_____
_____
_____

8) Unravel the problem with the **Supreme Court** decision of *Plessy v. Ferguson (1896)*.

_____

_____

_____

_____

_____

_____

9) What was the ruling of the **Supreme Court** case in *Brown v. Board of Education (1954)* and how did that upend *Plessy v. Ferguson (1896)*?

_____

_____

_____

_____

_____

_____

_____

_____

10) Describe some of the unintended effects of the ruling of *Brown v. Board of Education (1954).*

_____

_____

_____

_____

11) Outline the effects of the decision of **African American** woman **Rosa Parks** who refused to give up her seat on a bus in Montgomery, Alabama in 1955.

_____

_____

_____

_____

12) Rationalize why **Martin Luther King Jr**. and the **NAACP** got involved to help organize the **Montgomery Bus Boycott**.

_____

_____

_____

_____

_____

13) What did **President Eisenhower** do in order to enforce the *Brown v. Board of Education (1954)* ruling?

_____

_____

_____

_____

_____

The 1960s in America: Crash Course US History #40

1) Why were the **1960s** an important time in the **United States**?

_____
_____
_____
_____
_____

2) What was the purpose of the **Freedom Rides** on Greyhound buses?

_____
_____
_____

3) How did television help to make the **American** public aware of what was going on in the **"Jim Crow South?"**

_____
_____

4) Analyze the changes **Martin Luther King** called for in his **"I Have a Dream,"** speech in 1963.

_____
_____
_____
_____

5) Point out what **President John F. Kennedy (JFK)** realized about **racial inequality** in the **United States**.

_____
_____
_____

6) Explain what the **Civil Rights Act of 1964** prohibited in the **United States**.

_____
_____
_____

7) Disclose what the **Voting Rights Act of 1965** did to improve racial inequality.

_____
_____
_____
_____
_____
_____

8) Rationalize one of the **Socialist** ideas that **President Lyndon B. Johnson** set forth in his **domestic initiative** called the "**Great Society**."

_____
_____
_____

9) Elaborate the cause of the **Watts Riots** in **Los Angeles** during the **1960s**.

_____
_____
_____

10) What were some of the goals **civil rights** leader **Malcom X** wished to achieve for **African Americans**?

_____
_____
_____

11) Clarify why **anti-war protesters** protested against the **Vietnam War** (1955-1975) at the end of the **1960s**.

_____
_____
_____
_____

12) What did **Mexican-American** activist **Cesar Chavez** do to improve the working conditions of **migrant laborers**?

_____
_____
_____

13) Name some of the things that happened and changed the norms of society during the **American Feminist Movement** of the **1960s**.

_____
_____
_____

14) Interpret what rights the **Supreme Court** decision of *Roe v. Wade (1973)* guaranteed to **women**.

_____
_____
_____

15) Contemplate why **1968** such a society-changing year.

_____
_____
_____
_____
_____

The Rise of Conservatism: Crash Course US History #41

1) Show how there was a shift from the **liberal politics** of the **New Deal** to more **conservative politics** during the **1960s** and **1970s**.

_____
_____
_____
_____
_____
_____

2) Explain the shift in the **South** from **liberalism** to **conservatism** during the **Election of 1964** even though the presidency was won by **Democrat Lyndon B. Johnson (LBJ)**.

_____
_____
_____
_____
_____
_____

3) How did **Richard Nixon** win the **Presidential Election of 1968**?

_____
_____
_____
_____
_____
_____

4) What precedent did *Roe v. Wade (1974)* establish in the **United States**?

_____
_____
_____
_____
_____

5) Explain why **Title XI** was a victory for **working women**.

_____
_____
_____
_____
_____
_____

6) Why did **anti-ERA** promoters, such as **Phyllis Schlafly,** claim that **free enterprise** was the greatest liberator of **women**?

_____
_____
_____
_____
_____
_____

7) During the **Election of 1972**, why was the break-in of **Democrat Barry Goldwater's** campaign offices at the **Watergate** hotel so detrimental to **President Nixon**?

_____
_____
_____
_____
_____
_____

8) Why did **President Nixon** resign from office even though he may not have been part of the **Watergate** scandal?

_____
_____
_____
_____
_____
_____

9) Give concrete examples of the many things that **conservatives** found unsettling with **liberalism** in the **1970s** and why many saw it as a government out of control.

_____
_____
_____
_____
_____
_____
_____
_____
_____
_____
_____
_____

Ford, Carter, and the Economic Malaise: Crash Course US History #42

1) Describe the situation surrounding the **economy** in the **United States** during the **1970s**.

_____
_____
_____
_____
_____
_____
_____

2) Explain America's **trade export deficit** that began in 1971.

_____
_____
_____

3) Why didn't **President Richard Nixon's** strategy of taking the **United States** off the **Gold Standard** in 1971 work?

_____
_____
_____
_____
_____
_____

4) How did **globalization** in the **manufacturing** sector harm **American jobs** in the **United States?** (Include percentage figures per decade in your answer)

_____
_____
_____
_____
_____
_____

5) Explain what had happened to **industry** in the **Rustbelt Cities** around the **Great Lakes** region such as **Detroit** and **Chicago** by the **1980s**.

_____
_____
_____
_____
_____
_____
_____
_____
_____
_____

6) How did the **oil shocks** of the **1970s** send the **United States economy** into a tailspin?

_____
_____
_____
_____
_____
_____

7) Describe what happened to the **1970s economy** in the **United States** during **stagflation**.

_____
_____
_____
_____
_____
_____
_____

8) How did **President Jimmy Carter** try to tackle and solve the problem of **stagflation**?

_____
_____
_____
_____
_____
_____
_____

9) Justify or find faults with **President Jimmy Carter's Crisis of Confidence** speech.

_____
_____
_____
_____
_____
_____

10) Why do many people hold **President Jimmy Carter's** brokering of the **Camp David Accords** in 1978 as one of his greatest accomplishments?

_____
_____
_____
_____
_____
_____
_____

11) Put into words why the new theory of weakened support for **New Deal liberalism** in the 1970s led to the rise of a new way of **conservative economic** thinking.

_____
_____
_____
_____
_____
_____

## The Reagan Revolution: Crash Course US History #43

1) Why was **President Ronald Reagan** known as **The Great Communicator**?

_____
_____
_____
_____
_____

2) Outline what **President Ronald Reagan** meant by his version of "freedom."

_____
_____
_____
_____
_____
_____
_____

3) Elaborate on **Ronald Reagan's Economic Bill of Rights** program in 1987.

_____
_____
_____
_____
_____
_____
_____
_____
_____

4) Explain **supply-side economics**.

_____
_____
_____
_____
_____
_____

5) Identify and explain the major factor which caused the **national debt** to rise in the **United States** during the **1980s**.

_____
_____
_____
_____
_____
_____
_____

6) How did the **1980s** see a rising **inequality** between the poor, middle, and rich classes?

_____
_____
_____
_____
_____
_____
_____

7) Clarify the reasons behind how **President Ronald Reagan** ended the **Cold War** (1947-1991) between the **United States** and the **Soviet Union**.

_____
_____
_____
_____
_____
_____

8) Analyze the pros and cons of **President Ronald Reagan's Strategic Defense initiative (Star Wars)** during the end of the **Cold War** (1947-1991) in the **1980s**.

_____
_____
_____
_____
_____
_____

9) How did **President Ronald Regan** work with **Russian** counterpart **Mikhail Gorbachev** to reduce **nuclear missiles** during the **Cold War** (1947-1991)?

_____
_____
_____
_____
_____
_____

10) Describe in detail the biggest **scandal** during the **Reagan administration**.

_____
_____
_____
_____
_____
_____
_____
_____

George HW Bush and the End of the Cold War: Crash Course US History #44

1) Who was **George H.W. Bush** and how did he ascend to the presidency?

_____
_____
_____
_____
_____
_____

2) How did **Republican George H.W. Bush's** smear campaign in 1988 shape the outcome of the campaign of **Democrat Michael Dukakis**?

_____
_____
_____
_____
_____
_____
_____

3) Justify why the **end** of the **Cold War** (1945-1991) between **communism** and **capitalism** was positive for the world.

_____
_____
_____
_____
_____
_____
_____

4) Describe what happened at the **Malta Summit** in 1989 between US **President George H.W. Bush** and Russia's **Premier Mikhail Gorbachev**.

_____
_____
_____
_____
_____
_____

5) Explain the foreign policy surrounding the **Iraq War** in 1991, codenamed **Operation Desert Shield**, during the presidency of **George H.W. Bush**.

_____
_____
_____
_____
_____
_____

6) Why did **George H.W. Bush** lose his re-election bid even with his 89% approval rating six months before the **Election of 1992**?

_____
_____
_____
_____
_____
_____
_____

7) How did the **Rodney King** beatings in March of 1991 and the following trial cause the deterioration of white/black **race relations** in **Los Angeles**?

_____
_____
_____
_____
_____
_____

8) Describe the **civil unrest** that occurred in **Los Angeles**, California during the **Los Angeles Riots** in 1992.

_____
_____
_____
_____
_____
_____
_____

9) Analyze what happened to **Republican George H.W. Bush** after he **raised taxes** in 1992. Include the promise he broke to members of the **Republican Party** and why he broke his promise.

_____
_____
_____
_____

10) Define the **era America** was creeping up on as **George H.W. Bush's** presidency came to an end.

_____
_____
_____
_____
_____
_____
_____
_____
_____

The Clinton Years, or the 1990s: Crash Course US History #45

1) Briefly summarize **President William (Bill) Jefferson Clinton** administration's focus during the **1990s.**

_____

2) How did **terrorism** become a bigger issue during **Bill Clinton's** presidency?

_____
_____
_____

3) Analyze the success of the campaign of future **President Clinton** during the **Election of 1992**.

_____
_____
_____
_____
_____
_____

4) Describe the conundrum surrounding the "Don't Ask, Don't Tell," policy **President Clinton** supported for inclusion of **homosexual** members inside of the **military**.

_____
_____

5) Why didn't First Lady **Hillary Clinton's** proposed **1993 Health Care Initiative** that supported **universal health care** actually work?

_____
_____
_____

6) Outline the **Telecommunications Act of 1996.**

_____
_____
_____
_____

7) Briefly explain how the **Personal Responsibility and Work Opportunity Act of 1996** was seen as **President Bill Clinton's** signature **economic policy**?

_____
_____

8) How did the **personal computer** and the **internet** drastically change the **American economy** in the **1990s**?

_____
_____
_____
_____
_____
_____
_____

9) Explain how **Dot-com** companies led to the **Economic Crash of 2000**.

_____
_____
_____
_____
_____
_____

10) Describe what was going on with **immigration** between the years 1965 and 2000.

_____
_____
_____
_____
_____
_____

11) Point out how all of the **multiculturalism** and change in the **1990s** made for a very tense political atmosphere.

_____
_____
_____
_____
_____
_____

12) How was **President Clinton's** denial of a sexual relationship with **White House** intern **Monica Lewinsky** the basis for articles of **impeachment**?

_____
_____
_____
_____
_____

13) Give an explanation for how **globalization** in the **1990s** was pivotal to the world of the **21st century**.

_____
_____
_____
_____
_____
_____
_____

Terrorism, War, and Bush 43: Crash Course US History #46

1) Explain the controversy surrounding the **Electoral College** during the **Election of 2000**.

_____

_____

_____

_____

2) Analyze what happened in **Florida** during the **Election of 2000** which also played into the controversy of the **Supreme Court** decision of *Bush v. Gore (2000)*.

_____

_____

_____

_____

3) How did **environmentalists** view the **George W. Bush Administration's** non-cooperation with the **1997 Kyoto Protocol**?

_____

_____

_____

4) By what means did the **No Child Left Behind Act of 2001** reshape **education** in the **United States**?

_____

_____

_____

_____

5) Explain in detail what happened on **September 11, 2001**.

_____

_____

_____

_____

6) How did **civil liberties** in the **United States** change after **September 11, 2001**?

_____

_____

_____

_____

_____

7) Outline the **George W. Bush Administration's** policy, aka the **Bush Doctrine**, to expand the global **War on Terror**.

_____

_____

_____

8) Summarize the policies of the **USA Patriot Act of 2001**.

_____
_____
_____
_____
_____
_____
_____

9) What was the function of the **prison camps** in **Guantanamo Bay, Cuba**?

_____
_____
_____
_____
_____
_____
_____

10) Do YOU agree with the widespread phone-tapping **surveillance** of the **NSA (National Security Agency)**? Please explain YOUR position in detail.

_____
_____
_____
_____
_____
_____
_____
_____

11) Explain the **jobless recovery** of the economy after the **economic recession** in the years following 2001.

_____
_____
_____
_____
_____
_____
_____

12) How did **Hurricane Katrina**, which happened in 2005 during **George W. Bush's** second term as president, undermine the success of his presidency?

_____
_____
_____
_____
_____
_____
_____
_____
_____

Obamanation: Crash Course US History #47

1) What **economic** factors led to the **Great Recession** (2007-2009)?

_____
_____
_____
_____
_____

2) Outline the **subprime** money-lending factors surrounding a **NINJA loan.**

_____
_____
_____
_____

3) Why did **banks** think people would pay back their **NINJA loans**?

_____
_____
_____
_____
_____
_____

4) How did the United States **housing bubble of 2006-2008** turn into a full-fledged **economic crisis**?

_____
_____
_____
_____
_____

5) Explain what happened in the ensuing **Stock Market Collapse of 2008**.

_____
_____
_____
_____

6) How did **Barack Obama** win the presidency in the **Election of 2008**?

_____
_____
_____
_____
_____
_____
_____

7) Describe the **governmental reform** that **Barack Obama** achieved inside of his presidency.

_____

_____

_____

_____

_____

8) Evaluate the difference of opinion over whether **Obama's** economic **stimulus** policy, under the **Economic Recovery Act of 2009** passed by the **111 Congress**, actually worked.

_____

_____

_____

_____

_____

_____

9) Analyze the **Affordable Care Act of 2009,** aka **Obamacare,** and what it hoped to achieve.

_____

_____

_____

_____

_____

_____

10) Illustrate the concerns of the right wing **Republican** splinter group the **Tea Party**.

_____

_____

_____

_____

_____

_____

11) Outline the **political crisis** the **United States** faced during **Barack Obama's second term** as **POTUS (President of the United States)**.

_____

_____

_____

_____

_____

_____

12) In 21$^{st}$ century **America,** what does the **ideological** idea of **freedom** really mean?

_____

_____

_____

_____

_____

# Notes

# Notes

# Notes

# Notes

# Notes

# Notes

# Notes

# Notes

# Notes

# Notes

# Notes

# Notes

# Notes

# Notes

# Notes

# Notes

# Notes

# Notes

# Notes

# Notes

# Notes

Awesome Links:
John Green Crash Course US History Link:
https://thecrashcourse.com/courses/ushistory?page=2
or
https://www.youtube.com/watch?v=6E9WU9TGrec&list=PL8dPuuaLjXtMwme
pBjTSG593eG7ObzO7s

Free Primary and Secondary Reading Sources for Teachers of US History
https://sheg.stanford.edu/history-lessons

Pre-made flashcards for US History and Geography
https://quizlet.com/morante13

Make your own design for study review!
https://kahoot.it/

Awesome notes!
https://www.amazon.com/Everything-Need-American-History-
Notebook/dp/0761160833

Made in the USA
Middletown, DE
18 January 2022

59039167R00068